I0813359

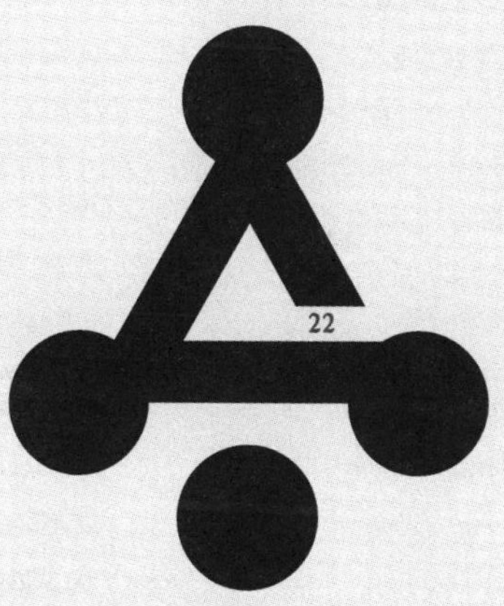
22

## Also by r.h. Sin

*Whiskey Words & a Shovel*

*Whiskey Words & a Shovel II*

*Whiskey Words & a Shovel III*

*Rest in the Mourning*

*A Beautiful Composition of Broken*

*Algedonic*

*Planting Gardens in Graves*

*Planting Gardens in Graves Volume Two*

*Planting Gardens in Graves Volume Three*

*She Felt Like Feeling Nothing*

*Empty Bottles Full of Stories*

*She Just Wants to Forget*

*Falling Toward the Moon*

*We Hope This Reaches You in Time*

*A Crowded Loneliness*

*She's Strong, but She's Tired*

*She Fits Inside These Words*

*Winter Roses after Fall*

*Dream, My Child*

*Anywho, I Love You*

*I Hope She Finds This*

*I Hope This Reaches Her in Time Revised Edition*

*Come Back to Me*

*This Day Is Dark*

*Beautiful Sad Eyes, Weary Waiting for Love*

*Ascending Assertion*

*A Midnight Moon*

*Read This If You've Been Ghosted*

*The Year of Letting Go*

*New Moons*

*My Dear Wildflower*

*Serenity's Song*

# THE QUIET AFTER

The authorised representative in the EEA is Simon and Schuster Netherlands BV, Herculesplein 96 3584 AA Utrecht, Netherlands. (info@simonandschuster.nl)

Andrews McMeel Publishing
a division of Andrews McMeel Universal
1130 Walnut Street, Kansas City, Missouri 64106

www.andrewsmcmeel.com

25 26 27 28 29 VEP 10 9 8 7 6 5 4 3 2 1

ISBN: 979-8-8816-0019-8

Library of Congress Control Number: 2025940539

Editors: Patty Rice and Danys Mares
Art Director: Diane Marsh
Production Editor: Elizabeth A. Garcia
Production Manager: Shona Burns

# THE QUIET AFTER
## POEMS OF HEALING SILENCE

r.h. Sin

22

after chapters
soiled in dirt
the fading of relationships
that could not work

i seem to have found
a joy, a peace
a solace, a space
that resembles sleep

an awakening happening
this moment is that
the sunlight found
a home through the cracks

my heart, left broken
but urged to heal
a cosmic dance
on quantum fields

a brilliant spark of light
in the form of a woman
a waltz through
the night sky like a comet

i see the heavens
in your eyes
the voice of God
in your essence

soft and powerful
like moonlight
out of this world
a nebulous awakening

you move through me
like a river in search of an ocean
you pull on me
like the moon tugs at the sea

it didn't work
because there's more
it didn't last
because there's better

what hurts now
will be the reason
your heart rejoices later

what's gone now
is just proof
that the best
is yet to come

there is a stillness
she's found

a point of clarity

a moment of refuge
within her own heart

self-love is healing her

self-love is helping her soul
rediscover its magic

self-love is guiding her
to a love that feels soft

they tell you
that you will never
find anyone like them

as if this healed
version of you
would ever want to be
with someone like them again

a soft life can't be cultivated
in a relationship with someone
who is confused about
their feelings for you

she moved into
the opposite direction
from the chaos
without speaking a word
because her silence
was more powerful
than any storm

peace was never handed to her
she built it from broken pieces
of her own heart
and wore it as a shield and armor

she was still
peaceful in her stature
because there is a power
in knowing that there
is never a need to fight
for what already belongs to her

she didn't even need to raise her voice
being loud wasn't necessary
her calm presence
was a quiet kind of flame
setting fire to everything
that didn't deserve her

her softness
was never weakness
it was proof
that she faced storms
and chose to bloom anyway

you see, walking away
isn't the end
it is the beginning

a choice to find peace
instead of staying
where you'll never be seen
or appreciated

never let them make you feel
like silence is surrender
sometimes peace
means calmly choosing yourself
removing your presence
to walk off into a hopeful silence
a new beginning

i didn't need a battlefield
to prove my strength
my calm resolve
the clarity i felt
was more than enough
to remind any storm
that i was untouchable

in the quiet dawn
of what was meant
to destroy her
she stands unbroken
a mountain embracing
the morning light

a moment of renewal
reflection, and rediscovery

her spirit hums gently
with the frequency of stars
cosmic, calm, and infinite

your strength flows
like a river
steady beneath the surface

she breathes peace
each exhale a whisper
of serenity and truth

beautiful vibrations
of courage
resonate within her
echoing through the void
dancing through the silence

through the static
her heart continues
to be a self-sanctuary
profound, still, and steady
a safe place for her essence

the light of the sun
the glow of the moon
dances on her resilient soul
breaking through the shadows

she rises on waves
of tranquility
anchored in strength
and self-love

that woman's essence
a shining light
radiating calm
she guides herself
through all adversity

tall, she stands
upon an unseen frequency
grounded while ascending

for she would not settle
for a love that didn't feel like
a soft, brilliant force of devotion

You see, she has entered into the era of
choosing herself, where her peace of mind
and heart will be nonnegotiable.

there is a beautiful freedom
in releasing what was never
meant to stay

like untangling yourself
from treacherous ropes

it's not a loss
it's reclaiming space
that was always yours

healing has never been loud
it's quiet in nature
gentle like a whisper in the void

a reminder that sometimes
the absence of someone
creates the greatest
sense of peace

removing someone
from your life
feels heavy at first
like breaking down
or breaking apart
but in the aftermath
of the silence that follows
you'll find pieces
of your heart
you didn't know
were missing

they were never your home
just a place in passing
and the emptiness they left
was a path, a doorway
to something more beautiful

I'm certain that you've been plagued with this belief that you lost them, but in truth, you found more of yourself in the spaces that were left to resemble a void. I found more of your truth in the silence, and in the end, you discovered the echoes of your own voice calling you back home.

You may find yourself in a slow season, and while you've been made to believe that slow is somehow boring and uneventful, you must understand that this tempo is your moment to plant seeds intentionally. This moment is your time to think about what you wish to manifest and to figure out what actions need to take place for your dreams to become tangible things.

There is a great power in being underestimated, especially by those who know you best. There is an inspiration that you can lock into deeply when the people in your presence lack the understanding and comprehension of your ability to overcome and further yourself to a destination that you've only realized within your dreams.

In my own experience, doubt has helped me evolve past the limitations imposed upon me by others. Doubt can be a beautiful fuel, for its texture is full of substance and life, depending on your mindset. You've been turning "can't do's" into "I can and I will" your entire life, so let this be a reminder that all things are possible whenever you're ready to make them possible.

What type of love would you experience if you weren't afraid of being alone? What type of love would be made possible if you refused to settle down in places that weren't fit for a heart like yours?

Don't let the past dictate the momentum of the present and the beauty that awaits you in the future. Don't give so much energy to what exists behind, and understand that moving forward without fear will grant you greater opportunities to find a love that will settle your heart in the softest of ways.

Somehow, loneliness was the cure. The thing that I was afraid of the most was always the medicine my heart and soul needed. So often, we run away from the silence that arrives after the ending of a relationship we believed would last. We see solitude as some sort of penalty for no longer being in a relationship, but we fail to realize that sometimes the lonely people on Earth are the ones who have never allowed themselves to be alone.

Being alone had eventually become a starting point for me. What is labeled loneliness can become a beautiful reference for what you'd like your life to be when shared with someone else. Being alone is a deep spiritual massage, a moment to recalibrate and to find bliss in practicing a level of self-love that will help you define the version of love that aligns best with your heart.

It has always been about energy. Life has always been a dance of what you give yourself to and what you refrain from interacting with. Sit in the stillness of the aftermath of everything that has happened in your life up until this moment and decide what no longer deserves your time, energy, and love.

The moment you decide that your
peace is more vital than controlling
external things, you reclaim
your time, power, and joy.

in this vast silence
everything is aligning
your thoughts and dreams
are finally embracing one another
in preparation for a meeting
with your soul
that will inspire the type of actions
to bring forth everything
you've been manifesting

refusing to play their game
is how you win

the war they've waged
upon your heart
has always been unnecessary
and a waste of your energy
don't react; that is where
victory will be discovered

She's been tending to old wounds with a newfound grace of compassion and self-love. This has been the beginning of an era where the healing is more focused and intentional.

Reaching that point in your life where you apply a deeper level of self-devotion by pouring more of yourself into all the places you previously neglected is so beautiful and profound. It's life-changing, and this is the era when you are ready to experience the actions that will produce the most life-changing results.

In this era of self-love and devotion, she has begun to set deep boundaries. She is in full understanding that the word "no" is a complete sentence and something she will not negotiate.

In this season of cultivating a
high vibration and leveling up,
she is letting go of all the things
that want to dim her light.

Let your actions speak of where you wish to go. May your actions align with your highest self as you continue to make beautiful choices that will usher you into an era of a beautiful life.

Queen, you've been shedding habits that no longer serve your highest self. You've been unlearning the things that have kept you from elevating and expanding. You, my love, are evolving into everything you were always meant to become.

SHE WILL NOT SETTLE FOR A LOVE THAT
ISN'T ROOTED IN NOURISHMENT. SHE IS
IN THE ERA OF MANIFESTING THE TYPE OF
ROMANCE THAT DEEPLY FEEDS HER SPIRIT.

an existence where my soul
is no longer confined
by the expectations of others

a life of emotional freedom
and soul rest
a place where my heart
is no longer in survival mode

Discovering strength in the absence of those who walked out of your life is a beautiful gift. There is so much clarity to be found in solitude. This is where you find your true awakening. This is the moment when the most beautiful transformations occur.

Allow self-love to lead your decisions. This is where heart-centered choices will be made. These are the moments that will move closer to a soft love that enables you to feel safe and calm.

You're beginning to trust the timing of the heartbreak that led you to this place of healing. This is your soul's awakening, the moment when you are faced with either the option to continue down a path that isn't yours or to decide to walk forward into a season of divine alignment. It's time for you to live within a reality that matches the brilliant light in your heart.

Right now, your need for survival is transforming into thriving. The pain you've felt for years is finally breaking up and being made into pieces that will come together to provide salvation and sanctuary. Just be patient with yourself.

I have always thought of you before I close my eyes to invite the silence of sleep. My mind gently races to this vision of you surviving circumstances that would have probably prevented others from pushing forward, but somehow you've always figured out how to outsmart the things that arrive to dumb down your existence or dim your light. You decide to shine despite the darkness hovering close above your head. You stand beneath a storm, dancing to the melody of raindrops, unafraid of the downpour because you see the rain as a cleansing and clearing. Your eyes are always fixated on a destination that aligns with what you wish your life to be, even while dragging yourself through mud that is put in place to slow down your pace. There's this indescribable strength in your fight; your will has allowed you to appear unstoppable even when breaking. And so, when I type up these words, an image of you sits at the center of my mind. Your very existence, soul, and persistence make for a beautiful poem, prose, and story. The way you live and love is legendary to me.

Her divine nature inspires the wind to blow, the clouds to rain, and the seasons to change. She speaks the language of transformation and renewal. She is you.

THIS IS A SEASON OF SELF-CONTROL, PATIENCE, REFLECTION, AND EMOTIONAL ENDURANCE.

in truth, i felt you
before i knew your name
like whispers written in the stars
like a song only my soul could comprehend

i would fall from heaven
just to sit in your presence
i'd trade eternity for the curve of your smile
for the way your eyes cause gravity to forget me

even if the world never sees us
even if time is for some reason unkind

i would choose you in every life
a stranger or my soul mate
a fleeting moment or forever

Through every moment of heartbreak, every setback, moments when the world attempted to dim your light, you have always burned brighter. You go from being a survivor to a brilliant force. A woman who knows that peace is not given but created . . . and healing is not waiting but deciding to go inward to practice self-love. Queen, your story is not written by the ones who tried to break you but by the way you continue to rise. Over and over again.

You know what . . . she has been the kind of woman who gave without keeping score, someone who has loved even when it hurt. She's been the woman who has stayed longer than she should have, hoping and believing, breaking down beneath the weight of unmet expectations, but she was never the problem. The ones she loved weren't ready for the kind of energy she carried.

She's done waiting to be seen by those too blind to appreciate her essence, presence, and worth. She finally sees herself, and that's enough.

Listen, I just wanted to say that you are not the brokenness they left behind. You are very much a storm that has learned to calm itself, the fire that refused to be extinguished. I want to remind you that healing isn't linear, but every step you take forward, even the smallest one, is a victory worthy of a beautiful celebration. You have survived many nights that have been darker than your doubts, and you have risen time and time again each morning with a heart brave enough to continue thriving. In truth, you are proof that pain can't bury beauty and that, even when love doesn't stay, you remain whole. Please, keep choosing yourself. You are the greatest love story you'll ever write, and the best chapters are yet to come.

It's strange the way you found the keys to unlock my light and my dark. The way you folded my pain gently and put me at ease. The way your heart ignited mine was just enough to remind me that love was necessary and possible.

Queen, the weight of your story sits in your bones, but it doesn't bend or break you. You carry both the tenderness and the ache, honoring each as part of the woman you are becoming. Even in silence, your spirit hums, a melody only those who've known both suffering and softness could ever understand.

You are not defined by the chaos that tried to consume you but by the grace with which you reclaimed yourself. Rooted and reaching. Soft but unshakable. You are proof that beauty can grow even in the darkest of places.

A struggle is not failure.

A GOOD WOMAN WILL ENRICH
YOUR PALETTE AND BROADEN YOUR
UNDERSTANDING OF LOVE AND LIFE.

last year, i healed
this year, i thrive

THAT WOMAN BECAME UNSTOPPABLE
THE MOMENT SHE REALIZED THAT
SHE COULD DO IT ALONE.

Choose the relationship that feels
like the relief of a deep exhale.

LOVING SOMEONE WITHOUT THE
FEAR OF GETTING HURT IS THE TYPE
OF FREEDOM I DESERVE.

Healing out loud because, for years, she suffered in silence.

slow success
slow love
slow life
slow, beautifully

The truth is, your evolution as a person will involve a lot of detachment from people and things, but the plus of it all is that you'll only lose the things that aren't worth keeping.

THIS IS THE SEASON WHEN YOU BEGIN
TO UNLEARN WHO THEY TAUGHT YOU
TO BE SO THAT YOU CAN GAIN A DEEPER
UNDERSTANDING OF WHO YOU ARE.

A woman who discovers that she is capable of becoming everything she needs will no longer settle in places that aren't worthy of her presence.

an abundance of harmony
will require the letting go
of all the people
who make you feel like
you're asking for too much
when what you want
is what you're willing to give

my love, your very existence
is the recipe for true love and magic
never settle

toxic energy is clearing
so that healthy things
can discover the spaces
available in your heart

what you deserve
is someone
who isn't distracted
by somebody
who isn't you

she's a seeker of everyday magic
and, eventually, she discovers
that she's been searching
for more of herself

She's enjoying the season between where she's been and where she's headed. She's sitting confidently between the life she's lived and the life she's been manifesting. She's healing between the moments, in deep rest, and practicing self-love daily.

This is the era when I trust the wisdom that my heart has gained from being broken. These are the moments in my life when my past is nothing more than a lesson, a place where my brilliance and strength were made greater so that I could continue forward, transforming the pitfalls into steps on the stairway to my greatest evolution. This next chapter of my life will be the most beautiful chapter I've ever written.

Letting go of you was a deep and beautiful apology to myself.

She's learning how to hold her fire. She is discovering how to dance with the beautiful flames in her heart, and she's burning away everything that isn't worth her energy.

There has always been this truly beautiful glimmer in your eyes, the way you look upon the world with this desire to experience it all and soak up the magic that lies hidden throughout the corners of this earth. I genuinely believe that you are attracted to magic because you've discovered that you are made from it. You search for the good in everything because you've discovered that inside you lives a deep kindness, and you require a level of softness because that is what resides in your heart, and so I see nothing wrong with you expecting the things you've desired from others. I don't think you've been asking for too much; I don't believe that you should be "realistic," as if to give up on this dream of love and devotion in your life. If anything, you should never settle for less than what you require. Especially when everything you seek is real, and the proof of that is your ability to give it to yourself.

I've lost that part of me that thrives on inner criticism of others. I must admit, in my time of anger, I'd often engage in these inner monologues about those who sought to trigger me, but one day, I woke up and began to move through life without that voice. Every time something went wrong or that person sought out a negative reaction, I could no longer find the words to utter, whether externally or inside my mind. This was the moment when I discovered that I had been set free from this need for that person to be a better version of themselves. You see, when you no longer feel the need to critique or react to the people who wish to disrupt your peace of mind, you are then free to move through your life unfazed in preparation for an eventual exit. The most beautiful thing about this is that your walking away is quiet and peaceful. Your walking away becomes a daily practice until, finally, you are no longer in a shared space with the things that do not align with the version of life you deserve to lead.

They want you to remain hurt because they
know that the moment you begin to heal
is the moment they become insignificant.

TURN YOUR LOVE INWARD AND THEY WILL
BECOME A MINOR FOOTNOTE IN YOUR STORY.

Your love is soft; you deserve soft love.

This is the era when you turn
survival mode off.

You deserve deep rest after all the
deep suffering you've experienced.

A soft life means letting go of people who
make you feel like you're too hard to love.

Burning bridges in the name
of peace of mind is a must.

A woman who understands that she's worthy of a love rooted in depth and softness will never settle just for the sake of being in a relationship.

Sometimes, choosing peace means
leaving that text on "read."

Never force love with a loser.
Your heart-shaped devotion will
never fit in the life of a square.

I look toward the night sky for a reminder of you and how bright you've been able shine during your darkest hours. Your strength is infinite, your love the depth of the ocean, and your soul a magic that most won't be able to comprehend. Baby, I see you clearly for all that you are, and I'm thinking about you tonight as you read these words.

Forgive me for all the times you searched for love and I wasn't there. You see, for years, I'd been looking for you in all the wrong the places, but, at last, this moment brings us closer together . . . Closer to the day when our fingers will meet and our palms will touch to cultivate a deep love and an infinite promise of pleasure, growth, prosperity, and peace. I'm sorry it took this long for me to love you.

EVENTUALLY, YOU LOOK AT THE PERSON
WHO HURT YOU AND LAUGH BECAUSE
YOU REALIZE THAT THEY WERE NEVER
WORTHY OF BEING FEARED.

One day, you'll leave behind the things
that you've outgrown, and this is when
the anger will become love once again.

SELF-LOVE IS THE HEART DECIDING
TO HEAL THE BODY.

This is the era when you begin to call
all of your power back to yourself.

You're not easily defined; your complexities are rooted in something so beautiful. Some will find it hard to comprehend the meaning of your presence, but there is someone who will get it on the first try, and I hope you never settle down until you find yourself in a relationship that mirrors the magic of everything you are.

you are the medicine
you are the cure
return to yourself
for healing

Queen, everything you touch
is bound to flourish
go inward if you're searching for gold
choose yourself if the decision
is meant to be magic

the woman who isn't afraid
to leave things behind
will always burn bridges
that lead back
to insignificant places
and or people

burning bridges
so that the things
left behind
have no way
of reaching me

all flowers bloom
some later than others
and that's okay

choosing to remain single
out of fear of settling
for a mediocre relationship

the abundance you seek
is already present
look inward

grow beyond the labels
and limitations
from those
who are threatened
by your evolution

the body is a home
the heart is a home
the soul is a home
the mind is a home

take care of yourself

what you allow
will be never-ending
write endings
for chapters
no longer worthy
of your attention

Let's normalize not addressing or acknowledging off-putting energy. Instead, silently put distance between yourself and people who know exactly what they're doing when they choose to trigger you.

Growth often looks like refusing to argue with people who are committed to their misunderstanding and or ignorance surrounding who you truly are as a person. Your character is not up for debate, especially with those who have placed limitations on who you can become.

The problem has been that you've been trying to get over an obstacle that is meant to be something that you easily walk around and pass, leaving it all behind with ease.

IT'S SAFE FOR YOU TO REFRAIN FROM GIVING
A FUCK ABOUT PEOPLE WHO DO NOT CONCERN
THEMSELVES WITH HOW THEY MAKE YOU FEEL.

Stop negotiating your value with people who can't afford to act appropriately in your presence.

DON'T SPEND ANOTHER YEAR OF YOUR
LIFE TRYING TO MEAN SOMETHING TO
SOMEONE WHO WILL NEVER BE CAPABLE
OF COMPREHENDING YOUR LOVE.

grow a plant
not a man

no longer bothered
by the things
that used to trigger me
no longer worried
about the people
who show no concern
or care about the way i feel

I no longer have the capacity to hate the way you lost me, and that alone is peace.

the body is capable
of rejecting someone's energy
pay attention, be mindful
and listen with your whole self

In this season of your life, you've chosen to avoid anything that may require you to become a reduced version of who you are. You no longer tolerate the things that require you to act out in low-vibrational ways.

You tolerate too many things when you fear losing people, but the moment you prioritize your peace overall, your boundaries become so strong that you naturally repel negative people and energy.

While I see the benefit of removing certain people from your life, taking it a step further and letting go of the person you felt you had to be in their presence is that much more powerful in redirecting your life onto the right path.

You have faced every moment of chaos in your life with your head held high and courage in your heart. There have been moments when you believed you couldn't go any further, and still that didn't keep you from going as far as you could to save yourself, and that's what I want you to remember whenever your world feels like it's falling apart. You can do this because you've always done so.

Stop forcing change in others. You must let a person be who they are so that you can decide where to put them in your life. The need to change others will cause the type of deep friction that will ultimately drain you of your energy. Accept the person in front of you for who they are, and decide whether or not they should be placed behind you as to be removed from your life.

Everything in your old timeline will struggle to reach you as you heal. The way you've been pouring back into yourself, the way you've chosen peace over holding on to the wrong things, the way you wake up each day with a heart filled with gratitude—these are the things that will help you in your ascension journey. The daily practice of nonreaction to the actions of people who don't care about you or your desire for harmony will push you to great heights. In the past, you turned your focus to urging those around you to change in ways that would benefit both parties. Still, at this moment, you arrive here with a heart full of acceptance and understanding that sometimes people will play themselves out of an opportunity to be a part of your life. All you can do is calmly say goodbye, because where you're headed, they're not meant to go. And that's okay.

A turning point for me was realizing my joy was restricted in many of my relationships. Where I had previously believed that having a companion would elevate my life, healing helped me discover that there is such a thing as being alone, even when in a relationship, and the ways one can literally feel as though they are serving out a prison term in a relationship that resembles an iron cage.

It's funny how we settle for a place that doesn't allow us to rest. A relationship should be a space of peace and harmony. Yet, we tell ourselves that the static and the chaos are normal because relationships can, at times, be filled with friction, tension, rage, and sadness. Still, when you begin to take those steps into healing and pour your love back into your heart, you find that a relationship can be a safe space. A relationship can be a home that feels like a sanctuary or a paradise; it should be a place where one returns to feel joy and inspiration. You realize this can be real because you are cultivating this within yourself each and every day. The relationship you forge with yourself goes on to define the type of relationship you long to enter.

When I began my self-love journey, I realized just how wrong I was in my choosing of a partner. It's a tough thing to grapple with, a truth that has led me down paths of hurt and destruction, but in the end, every crack in my heart became a line of inspiration for me to cultivate from within all the things that I couldn't find in others. I feel that maybe you feel this as well. How your past has led you to moments of deep reflection and strengthened your desire for great change. I have come to love the ways that someone's lack of care or hatred toward me somehow provided a metaphorical map for me to follow, and the irony is that the pain they caused only helped me become strong enough to know that the true power is not in fighting them back but in walking past them because they no longer serve a purpose in my story.

remember yourself
the way you moved freely
the way your heart felt calm
even as it longed for another

remember the way you laughed
loud, big, unapologetically
the way you wore a smile
the way your eyes
held a joy
that made your face light up

remember the ways
you dreamed about love
the way it should be
the things you'd require
and deserved

remember the way you were
before you fell for someone
who wanted to dim
the light in your soul

and know that it is possible
to find your way back
while moving forward

in leaving you
i returned to me

My life dramatically changed when I realized that we often return to patterns and habits that are rooted in familiarity. The problem with this is that if all you've known is pain, misfortune, and chaos, you find yourself choosing this over and over, a cycle of worthlessness and despair. But if you begin to alter what's familiar, day by day, you transform the quality of those patterns by increasing the quality of your habits. Your actions each day can literally alter what you view as familiar by making healthier choices. It won't be easy, but living a life plagued by sadness isn't easy either. And so, because you made it this far, I know that you can do this as well. You are capable of great change, and the proof will always be the fact that you have survived everything that was meant to destroy you. And now you will choose to do what brings you peace.

you are a lotus
rising from the mud
choosing to thrive
choosing to bloom

your soul
has been
whispering
the truth

be alone
and listen

the moon
has no expectations
of the sun

she sits freely
in the night sky
shining her light
into the shadows

she looks into the darkness
unafraid and calm
a slow dance
steady into
the morning light

she is you

this season of healing
feels like an autumn day
letting things fall
to make room for
something new
and beautiful

What I can tell you about the love that arrives in the midst of inner work is that it challenges you to go deeper, inspires a greater understanding of the soft tranquility that can be found in self-love, and remains proof of the work you've done for yourself because you find that you are now attracting from a frequency that feels safer, certain, and free. What I can say about the love that finds you while you're busy finding yourself is that it's unlike anything you've ever experienced, and it leaves you questioning why you didn't begin this healing process earlier.

You see, so much of what comes is representative of something that people claim is nonexistent, but here it is, standing in front of your heart, ready to share in the peace you've cultivated, prepared to share in the love that has been made capable out of your desire to heal from everything that has taken place in your past.

What I can tell you about the love that arrives in the midst of inner work is that it will be the greatest love you've ever experienced, simply made possible by the daily practice of loving yourself deeply.

This love will remind you of those initially tender feelings you experienced during your first interactions with how you hoped love to be. It'll feel pure and untainted. Safe and inspirational. This love will seem alien because, over the course of your life, these feelings were made to be unfamiliar, but eventually you'll go on to remember it as the version of love your heart has always deserved but was unable to find due to the restrictions created by ignoring the traumas of your life.

I want this for you because I have seen it for myself. I have touched the texture of what it feels like to be reintroduced to a love that is healthy and safe. I want this for you because life is too short to go on fighting for love beside a person who only wants to go to war with you.

you see, the heart
is but a garden
sometimes fed
by your own tears
and brought to bloom
in moments of solitude

stay loyal
but never
betray yourself

THIS IS THE ERA WHEN YOU SUCCESSFULLY DISCOVER MORE OF THE LOVE YOU SOUGHT OUT IN OTHERS INSIDE YOUR OWN HEART.

Refuse to be reduced by people
who can't comprehend the value of
what you bring into their lives.

sometimes the grass
isn't greener
it's just artificial

you have become the story
of what happens
when a rose
decides to bloom
during a drought

keep growing

a woman
embracing
the fullness
of her magic
is the sweetest poem
ever written

sometimes
you have to leave
to walk into
your own embrace

give extreme focus
to the things
that make
your heart smile
and that soak your soul
in peace

the universe
will make you wait
when it intends
to give you more
than you expected

be patient

real conversations
with genuine souls

In this season of my life, I am keeping my mental well-being sacred and safe from the noise of those who wish to speak chaos and unrest upon me.

IT'S THE MAGIC OF DECIDING TO WAIT FOR
THE TYPE OF LOVE THAT OTHERS HAVE LOST
THE PATIENCE AND COURAGE TO BELIEVE IN.

holding a grudge
is the choice
to hold on to darkness
that isn't yours

let it go
free yourself
to welcome love
and peace

the more you know
who you are
the easier it becomes
to burn down bridges
that won't take you
to where you wish to be

There is a power in saying nothing even while there is so much to be said. When you master acts of silence, you discover true peace of mind.

same garden
but some
grow faster
than others

Sometimes, you have to take control of your desire to have closure by choosing to accept who a person is and the way they've acted. Sometimes, their decisions and how they made you feel are all the closure you'll ever need.

nostalgia is nice
but the future is beautiful

The moment you alter the way you view yourself and your life, the sooner your future will evolve into something you could never imagine. The direction of your life is rooted in the way you think about it.

Once you realize that it's not you and that the person who is attempting to disrupt your flow of peace is just an individual who has yet to take accountability for their issues, you can move through this earthly realm unbothered and free from carrying the burden of someone else's inability to cope with their pain. In the course of your life, you will find yourself in several situations in which people will make themselves to be an opposition to everything you want to experience, but in stillness, in mindfulness, and in being self-aware, the truth of what you're up against will be made clear to you each and every time.

I've come to this realization that most of the people I've shared spaces with have a hard time self-regulating. Having kids and spending the majority of my time present in the raising of toddlers helped me see the immaturity and undeveloped parts within the adults who have become agents of chaos, people who have attempted to disrupt the flow of joy and peace within my own life. While this conclusion has given me the type of insight to maybe share some compassion with those individuals, still, we all have a choice in how we want to interact with the world and with others.

When you fully see a person for who they are at their core, you can practice a level of acceptance that makes it easier to move around whatever obstacles they place in your path. And that's how I've been able to maintain a sense of calm; this is how I've gotten better at protecting my peace.

Accept them for who they are and decide what level of attention you're willing to give. Maintain a level of accountability for how much energy you give this person, and if your energy is wasted on these individuals, let them go and remove yourself. Life is too short to engage in some sort of warfare with people who are actually at war with themselves. Life is too short not to take advantage of the peace you can readily cultivate within by detaching from people who are not willing to do the necessary inner work.

This idea and the actions that have followed have helped me discover a world within our world. It's almost as if everything in existence is alive on a timeline, and with every discovery you make, you change your external world because you decide not to put up with behaviors that push you further from your destination in terms of what you wish to feel. The beautiful thing about this is that, even in a shared space, your reluctance to engage with someone who wants to pull you out of character creates a sort of barrier or forcefield, protecting you from whatever they want to throw in your direction.

Over the years, there have been blockages in your life in the form of people, and you've learned that, in order for blessings to move freely through your life, you've had to let them go.

You mustn't forget this.

Give yourself a bit more credit
for how you saw the rainstorms as
food to nurture your growth.

It is beautifully profound to witness a woman unfold and release her sadness and fears to make room for peace, happiness, and genuine connections rooted in deep love.

You just have to remember that someone's inability to love you in the ways you need is not a reflection of your worth.

TO REACH THE END OF ANYTHING,
STILL BELIEVING IN SOMETHING
BEAUTIFUL AND DEEP, IS A TRIUMPH.

i walk through Central Park
mid-autumn, a full heart
remembering that the leaves
are falling to give way to new life
and it is here that the end
takes the form of the beginning

being sensitive
is not a weakness
it takes great strength
to feel so deeply

it took me so long
to see this place
for its restrictive nature

many nights
i lie a restless
prisoner
with nowhere to go
or so i thought

the key to this cage
was me all along
and acts of self-love
set me free

don't be so obsessed
with the future
that you forget
that you are surrounded by
all the things you manifested

know the difference
between a garden
and a grave

THE HEALTHIER THE MIND, THE MORE
IT REFUSES TO GOSSIP. SPEAKING ILL
OF OTHERS IS CANCEROUS TO PEACE.

You are worthy of everything
you've dreamed about.

she's tough enough
to stay soft

the silence of a calm woman
is a roar to the man
who's lost her for good

go where
your heart
has the greatest chance
at being appreciated

she is forged in fire
rebirthed, stronger
wiser, more beautiful
at the end
of every disaster

when they look at her
human eyes
they're unaware of
what they've seen
because whatever
she's made of
is not from this world

stop fighting
for the things
you should discard

you are so luminous
go only where your light
is encouraged
to burn brighter

Trust the process. Sometimes,
a thing needs to break to be
rebuilt better and stronger.

break the pattern
rewire the heart
end the cycle

learn to remain calm
when the disrespect
is heavy

walk away from people
who are inadequate
in their behavior
toward you

set your frequency
to self-love
and witness the magic
within your own body

your healed self
is coming
to save
your inner child

she paints her life
in colors
that have yet
to be discovered

this is why
they can't comprehend
what they see
when they see her coming

reclaiming my energy
reigniting my heart

love, don't confuse yourself as a sacrifice
when you have always been the altar

you were assigned that heartbreak
as proof that you are deserving
of your love more than anyone else

you are the before
and the after
everything between
was just a lesson

let them think
whatever they wish
you are not at war
with the lies
people tell about you

go slower
in the activities
that make
your soul happy

warmth is soothing
to the nervous system

a warm conversation
a warm embrace
a warm love

she's not lucky
she's aligned

respond differently
to the problem
and the cycle
will break

she could not
accept limitations
because she knew
her soul was infinite

Sometimes, triumph feels like being
in the middle of a struggle.

In the morning, think about how far you've come, and focus on the type of life you wish to experience. Cultivate a sense of gratitude for all that you have, and think fondly about the beautiful things that are possible based upon all the beautiful things that are currently in your life at that moment.

Happiness is a choice, and the choice must be made upon waking up each morning. Choose to pour your energy into things that result in laughter and emotional prosperity. Do things that are beneficial to your health, both physically and mentally. Operate daily from a place of self-love and genuine care for others and your entire reality will change for the better.

this day will never happen again
and tomorrow, you could be different
slow down and be with yourself
in this moment

worrying about a narcissist
is like worshipping the problem
pay no mind to the mindless
waste no energy on insignificant things

let go of the need
to do and be more
for someone
who is comfortable
with giving you less

alone is where
you keep yourself warm
it's where loneliness
becomes a fire

i am grateful
for all the things
that happened
before this moment
to lead me to a place
of deeper understanding
of myself and my desires

i am ready
for what comes next
i am open
to the good
that is to arrive
into my life

i am prepared
to use all the lessons
that the trauma, the sadness
the heartbreak
have taught me
i am ready to apply
everything i've gained
to welcome more abundance
and blessings into my life

i am healing continuously
i am practicing self-love daily
and i am beginning to remember
every bit of myself that i thought
was lost due to the tragedies
that have found me
over the course of my life

i am ready, i am ready
i am ready

you are fully capable
of giving life
to the things in your mind

you turn your dreams
into tangible experiences
you pull your thoughts
into the physical world

that is your gift

she is both soft as sheep and wild as wolves
she's mastered the balance of being a woman

This is the season when you refuse to shrink yourself to make others feel more comfortable with your presence.

I HOPE YOU LEARN THE MAGIC AND
POWER OF CULTIVATING A LIFE THAT
YOU DON'T NEED TO ESCAPE FROM.

a woman who has decided
to invest her energy
into the prosperity
of her mind, body, and heart
will no longer entertain
unhealthy relationships
and conversations

peace at all costs
i'm ready to lose anything
and anyone who stands
in the way of my bliss

silently building a foundation
for inner wealth

think of what matters
most to your soul
then prioritize that

It's so easy to blame others, but I want you to remember that there is a great deal of freedom waiting in the decision to embrace accountability. Yes, people will act in harmful ways against you, but in the end, reclaiming your choice to tolerate or walk away from these people will always be up to you. Do not give your power away by holding grudges against people who lack self-control. Do not waste your life focusing on what has been done to you for too long. Learn the lesson in heartache and apply it to every decision you make afterward. See how much you level up in ways that will make it impossible for the wrong people to get in your way.

she knows her worth
she knows when and where
to provide her presence
she knows her power
and where best to use it
she knows her value
and what to do
when she is not appreciated

she's existing in her full energy
a cosmic woman
pulling from a source
that is otherworldly

today, i wake up lighter
today, a little bit closer
to freedom

after all that i've survived
i am more me
than i've ever been

i am wiser
than i ever was
and stronger
than i thought
i could be

today, i claim victory
in this moment
i am triumphant
over everything
and anyone
with bad intentions

today, i free myself
from shame and guilt
i free myself
from low-vibrational feelings
and thoughts
i free myself from the expectations
and judgment of others

No matter the obstacle, you always see yourself through. Nothing can keep you from shining; even on your darkest days, your light can't be diminished. And while this year might have been a tough one, each day, you become stronger, wiser, more you, more magic.

Genuinely proud of you and your ability to overcome all obstacles on this journey in healing past wounds.

REFUSING TO BE PULLED INTO UNNECESSARY CONFLICT IS A BEAUTIFUL FLEX.

Peace is something you can always access by going inward. Peace is something you can sustain when you refuse to entertain people whose main intent is to trigger you. Look at your life and who makes things difficult for you to get through the day, and silently begin the process of removing that person or those people.

There is something beautiful awaiting you on the inside of your heart. When you have that desire for love, please, by all means, venture inward, because you are capable of giving yourself everything that others refuse to.

While none of us are perfect, there are people who exhibit a cycle of behavior that will often sour their own experiences in life while also leaving a path of emotional destruction as they venture off into their own oblivion. If you are with someone who wants you to carry on in their misery, let them go. Let them find out what life has in store for them. You process the experience, heal, and love yourself. GOOD THINGS ARE COMING. I'm right there with you.

At the very start, you're hurt and angry, but eventually you may realize that the person who hurt you just made you stronger. In the end, they are nothing but a lesson, a footnote on your journey to genuine and lasting love.

I think it's important to understand that you are fully responsible for your joy, your peace, and everything you wish to feel. There is a power in understanding that you get to decide and that no one can make you feel anything without your permission, and so the moment I began to say no to the things that made me feel bad or angry, my life began to change, bit by bit. And while I'm not completely healed, I walk through the day with an ease and a momentum that sets me 100 steps ahead of anything or anyone who may want to bring me down. You hold the power, and I hope this reminds you to take it back.

Someone told me that if you become the love you desire, you will attract the love you deserve.

This is true. Become a better you and you will attract better things. Better experiences. Better love. Better friendships.

Peace is something that you can build up as a reserve. The more you learn how to best interact with the external world, the more beautiful your inner world becomes. So that when something disruptive occurs in your life, it is much easier to return to that baseline to access the peace you've cultivated over time.

I think sometimes you forget how special you are. There's a loyalty in your heart that can't be diminished. A fire in your presence that can't be put out. You are brilliant in your emotional intelligence, but it's just that the people you've met have not been able to see beyond the surface and, in a way, that's fine, because you're not meant for everyone.

This is me saying I see you and I appreciate the energy you put out into the world.

The biggest freedom lies in letting go.

The greatest clarity can only be achieved once you place distance between yourself and those who attempt to muddy your energy.

The probability of good things occurring happens once you decide to break free from toxic cycles and people.

This is your reminder to let go.

Lean in to this idea that you deserve a life that isn't filled with drama, tension, and problematic behavior.

It all starts in the mind. That belief will push you toward the actions that will help you cultivate the life you've dreamed of.

There is so much power in accountability. This is how you move on; this is how you evolve.

You've been through it, time and time again; you've displayed a great knowledge in survival, but it's time to thrive.

Your moment is coming; just be patient. While I hate the fact that you've gone this long feeling this way, it is important to remember that, when obstacles stand in the way of everything you wish to feel, you figure out how to become stronger, wiser.

You are an incredible experience, and every day you happen to yourself. A blessing, a beautiful gift. A soul worth loving. A heart to be adored.

Don't settle.

Trust that the universe will remove the wrong things from your life just as long as you continue to make the right choices regarding your life.

We never realize just how often we project the things we want onto people who don't even have the ability to offer or share in the right forms of energy. I think the longing for a companion becomes so deep that we choose anyone as the one, and we paint them up in the colors of our desires and hopes. The red flags are big and red everywhere in the beginning, but we've decided that every transgression that happens in the honeymoon phase is acceptable. We ignore the logic and the reason and hold on to this rush of endorphins that happens, not because this person is the one but because this person is just something new, and the heart tends to get excited about the possibilities that reside within a new experience.

Then the roller coaster begins and, unlike the ones in a theme park, the ups and downs here are genuinely detrimental to our future because, eventually, it feels like a ride from hell that won't let you off. Every moment spent seated in that car going nowhere is another moment in time that could have been spent walking toward your destiny.

This realization didn't really dawn on me until I was asked the simple question of "why" as it pertained to why I kept picking the "wrong" mate. I had been choosing my partners from an unhealed space in my heart that would cause me to pick a person who didn't align with what I wanted in a partner. Now, the most important thing here was understanding that what I said I wanted was disconnected with the act of choosing, because these things can only ever truly line up when the wounds from the past have healed. It's like the closing of this both emotional and mental gap, a bridge being cultivated, so that both ends can produce the result one claims to desire.

I've been saying this to anyone who would listen, and because you're reading this book right now, I know you may need this as well. Please, heal your relationships. Take steps in healing at the root of who you are so that a wiser, stronger you can then emerge and properly help lead you to the right paths that will take you on a healthier journey to everything you believe you deserve.

The unrest you've experienced in your soul is more than likely because you've yet to properly release the things that are unnecessary to continue to carry. The choices you make are at times related to the choices you've made before, and it's time to stop letting the past dictate so much of your today and tomorrows. It's time to welcome a stillness into your life. It's time to experience a softer form of existing, and I hope you return to these words whenever you feel a struggle in your chest and head.

After everything you've experienced in your life, after everything you've survived, it's time to live a little bit more gently. It's time to put down the armor and sword for just a moment.

It's time to rest in the quiet that exists after the storm.